Workbook Four
Of the Business Essentials Series

HOW TO GENERATE
MORE CLIENTS PROFITABLY

John Millar

Copyright © 2016 John Millar
All rights reserved. No part of this publication may be reproduced, distributed, or transmitted in any form or by any means, including photocopying, recording, or other electronic or mechanical methods, without the prior written permission of the publisher, except in the case of brief quotations embodied in critical reviews and certain other noncommercial uses permitted by copyright law
All rights reserved.

ISBN: 1535120878
ISBN-13: 9781535120876

DEDICATION

I dedicate this book to my mother and father, who raised me while self-employed. They taught me to work hard and listen to everyone but to make my own choices as to what is right and what is wrong.. and oh, did I mention work hard?

Anyone who tells you to work smart not hard hasn't ever done it tough and realized that if you work smart AND hard you will achieve more than you can possibly dream.

CONTENTS

	Dedication	i
1	Product Description	Pg 1
2	Workbook Content	Pg 2
3	7 Steps to More Profit in Less Time	Pg 37
4	The Business Essentials Series	Pg 18
5	About the Author	Pg 41
6	Client Testimonial	Pg 42

PRODUCT DESCRIPTION

If there are no clients from whom to generate income, there becomes little point in carrying on a business. We all know how important the generation of new clients can be. And we know too that outgoings spent on advertising can have hit and miss results.

That's why at More Profit Less Time, we dedicate serious time and energy into training our business owners in familiarizing themselves with the factors that generate more clients as opposed to actions that simply stimulate the bank accounts of advertisers.

You will learn:

1. How to develop your unique placement within your industry
2. How to create a compelling and risk-free guarantee
3. The basics of good, measurable advertising
4. The difference between advertising and effective marketing
5. How to extract the greatest value from the least outlay
6. How to continue to prosper in difficult economic times

The essential pointers that you will evaluate and assess within this module are priceless in what they can do for your business. If you're looking for the best ways in which to capitalize on what you have, whilst still expanding your business, then this is the DVD for you.

Regards,

John Millar

In business it's all about having your marketing work for you and get a strong return on your investment of time and money and achieve great things inside your business.

So what is marketing?

....

....

....

....

The essence of marketing is all about communication, inspiration, and education.

> You must communicate effectively and efficiently with those that you wish to communicate with while inspiring them to have what you offer and educating them as to why they need it. Remember that people buy based on the emotions they feel then justify their purchase with the logic that they think. – John Millar

....

....

....

....

You must present your marketing so its appealing to both sides of the brain which are the logical and emotional / creative.

....

....

....

....

....

....

....

> We need to let people know what's available from YOU. What the benefits they will gain by doing business with YOU. What they can buy from YOU. How to choose what YOU have to offer, and then how and why they need to buy from YOU.

_____
_____
_____
_____

I believe that unless you've created or present as having the most unique product or service in the marketplace then you are setting yourself up to attract shoppers and not raving fans.

> What is that major differentiator you have that is going to determine whether or not they make a purchase from YOU?

1. _____

2. _____

3. _____

> What is it that makes YOU and YOUR business special that no one else in your industry can

1. _____

2. _____

3. _____

Marketing's not just about advertising. Advertising is merely a portion of marketing.

Marketing starts well before the purchase begins and continues well after the sale.

_____
_____
_____

HOW TO GENERATE MORE CLIENTS PROFITABLY

> What can you do inside your business to make sure you get your half and half right? Where your half is your distribution and the other half is the marketing. Because there's no use marketing and promising something that you can't deliver.

1.
2.
3.
4.
5.

> What are you doing to make sure that your distribution and your marketing match up together so that you can deliver consistently in a manner that under promises yet over delivers?

1.
2.
3.
4.
5.

Marketing is only profitable when it's no longer viewed as an expense but when it's viewed as an investment.

I believe that unless you've created or present as having the most unique product or service in the marketplace then you are setting yourself up to attract shoppers and not raving fans.

> So what is the definition of an investment? In fact I think there are two definitions we need to consider here.
>
> 1. In finance, the purchase of a financial product or other item of value with an expectation of favorable future returns. In general terms, investment means the use of money in the hope of making more money.
> 2. In business, the purchase by a producer of a physical good or intangible service in the hope of improving future business.

You must demand the simple expectation of getting a return on our investment in all of your marketing and the only way to make sure of that is to constantly test and measure everything.

You've heard me say it before but unless you test and measure these things within the business, how do you know that you've made an intelligent marketing decision?

HOW TO GENERATE MORE CLIENTS PROFITABLY

How would you like to actually have an unlimited marketing budget?

....

....

....

....

....

....

....

What we need to do to get an unlimited marketing budget is first and foremost understand what our acquisition cost is.

....

....

....

....

....

....

....

How much does it cost me or how much am I prepared to invest to get one new customer?

....

....

....

....

....

....

....

JOHN MILLAR

You MUST know your numbers from the 7 Steps to More Profit In Less Time Worksheet to even think about making this decision.

7 Steps to More Profit Less Time

Area	Current Figure	Areas of Potential	Increase	New Forecast
Number of Enquiries	4,000	Host Beneficiary, Strategic Alliance, Website SEO, Networking Groups	10%	4,400
×				×
Conversion %	25%	Defined USP, Quality Guarantee Sales Training, CRM	10%	27.5%
=				=
New Customers	1,000			1,210
+				+
Retained Customers	2,000	Members Kit, Newsletters Customer Surveys, Loyalty Program	10%	2,200
=				=
Total Customer Base	3,000			3,410
×				×
Average $ Sale	$100	Increase Prices, Use a checklist Offer Finance, Upsell and Cross Sell	10%	$110
×				×
Average of Transaction	2	Have an engaged database, Sell more consumables, Build a relationship	10%	2.2
=				=
Total Revenue	$600,000			$825,220
×				×
Average GP Margin %	25%	NO DISCOUNTING, Reduce Waste, Negotiate better trading terms, Measure everything	10%	27.5%
=				=
Total Gross Profit	$150,000			$266,935.20
−				−
Fixed Costs	25%	Better time management, Systemize the routine, Reduce Duplication	10%	$90,000
=				=
Net Profit	$150,000			$136,935.50

www.moreprofitlesstime.com | www.ceo-ondemand.com

So often I see clients and they've run the same ad week in, week out which can be great because consistency in your advertising is one of the most important things you can do. You must get a balance between creating something memorable so it stands out and keeping things like your branding and style the same so it's comfortable and relates to you and your business.

– John Millar

What is your current cost of acquisition?

Are you getting a greater return than what you're spending?

Do you know what the lifetime value is for your average client?

As an example of acquisitive v lifetime value of a client for a coffee shop:

Investment on advertising:	$1,000 per week
New customers gained:	10
Average spend from those new customers:	$5.50

What is my cost of acquisition?

What is the lifetime value of my new clients?

Was this a good investment?

What happens when we start looking at the same scenario but in a different and thinking of the lifetime value of our clients and tie in the 7 Steps to More Profit In Less Time so you test and measure every step of the process?

Investment on advertising:	$1,000 per week
We now measure the new enquiries:	20

We improve our conversion rate by 10%

New customers gained:	11

With better customer service and sales skills we improve the average dollar sale by 10%

Average spend from those new customers:	%6.05

We now measure how often they come in and buy each week (number of transactions)

Purchases each week:	2

We now test and measure how many weeks the average client will stay a regular client

Average weeks a client is retained:	52

We also set up an active series of activities that proactively drive and measure referrals

Number of referrals per year on average:	12

What is my cost of acquisition?

What is the lifetime value of my new clients?

Was this a good investment?

Not only does this way of thinking change our whole mindset to marketing and advertising but it allows you to stop the revolving door of customers, improve client retention and improve your business as a whole!

Take a few minutes, work out the math of the lifetime value of your clients if you look after them properly, had them staying longer, spending more and more often and referring people to you!

HOW TO GENERATE MORE CLIENTS PROFITABLY

What are the 10 strategies you need to implement in your business to start measuring and improving your lifetime value with every single client?

1.
2.
3.
4.
5.
6.
7.
8.
9.
10.

How much are you now prepared to invest to gain a new client?

What is the average lifetime value of your current clients?

What can you do to add real value to your new and current clients?

I believe that you know you are giving enough value when it starts being painful, then give a little bit more so you are giving

What is your USP, Unique Selling Point?

What should you have as a USP and guarantee?

....
....
....
....

What should you have as a USP and guarantee?

....
....
....

Why should you create a powerful guarantee?

....
....
....
....

The easiest way to get started here is to answer a few questions, just to get you thinking.

To come up with a powerful guarantee, you need to know what your customers want you to guarantee, and what you actually can promise.

The idea is to match your abilities with your customers' wants.

Often, it's a good idea to over promise, it'll make you pick up your act, and probably be more in line with your current customers' perceptions anyway.

....
....
....
....
....

HOW TO GENERATE MORE CLIENTS PROFITABLY

Here are the questions you must answer to create a truly meaningful USP and Guarantee...

What is your current guarantee?

What are 3 problems or frustrations buying your product/service solves?

1.

2.

3.

What frustrations do customers experience when trying to find your product or service?

What frustrations do customers experience when they go to buy your product or service?

What are the 3 major benefits of buying your product or service?

1.

2.

3.

What frustrations do customers experience when using your product or service?

What frustrations do customers experience after they've bought your product or service (e.g. - lack of after-sales service)?

If you were a customer, why would you dislike buying from you?

HOW TO GENERATE MORE CLIENTS PROFITABLY

Describe the sort of potential customers who love buying from you ... and why?

If you could easily overcome any 2 of your customers frustrations what would they be and how would you overcome them?

1.

2.

3.

What 6 things that will relieve your customer's frustrations that you can guarantee, and deliver 100% of the time right now?

1.

2.

3.

4.

5.

6.

What 3 additional things will you be able to fully guarantee within the next 3 months?

1. ....

2. ....

3. ....

List 3 things that you can NOT confidently guarantee today, that you would love to be able to guarantee tomorrow...

1. ....

2. ....

3. ....

What is the ONE thing that, if you could guarantee it, would make you the market leader? (For example, a news agency that guarantees to sell you a winning lottery ticket every time). Is there any way in the world, within the realms of human possibility, that you could

....

....

....

....

....

....

> If it makes you unique it also has to be something that is more than a little bit scary, it has to be almost terrifying or you are not truly unique you are another "Me Too" and the only thing you can differentiate on is price! – John Millar

It must be something that's so exciting that it gets other people talking.

_____
_____
_____
_____

Why do we want other people talking?

We want them talking because they are now providing us with free marketing and advertising and whether they know it or not, they're not only advocating your products and services, they're promoting you, your products and your services to other people for FREE. They've now become your unpaid sales team and an unpaid marketing and advertising source for you.

This is how you create an unlimited marketing budget.

_____
_____

If you had a great experience did you tell other people about it?

_____
_____

Likewise, if you've had a poor experience I'm sure you've told lots of people out there as well.

_____
_____
_____

> Remember, your USP and guarantee can't be something that can be easily copied. It can't be an obvious rip-off. Uh, It can't be something that's just another me-too otherwise it's not a unique selling point.

It also allows you the opportunity now to force your business to achieve a state of excellence.

To achieve that accelerated state where your competition are left behind and kept left behind.

> What are the easiest – from easiest to hardest, things that you can actually do to be truly unique in, in your market. Write them down and also grade them from the cheapest to the most expensive things.

1.
2.
3.
4.
5.
6.
7.
8.
9.
10.

> We want you to look at the cheapest and easiest things that you can do straight away and plan later for the hardest and most expensive things that are actually going to achieve that offer a return on investment for you.

Get 80% right and then make it happen, remember Procrastination Is A Wealth Hazard.
– John Millar

> What are some of the biggest myths about guarantees that hold themselves back?

Firstly, most people are genuinely terrified of is that they just physically can't do it. They're not capable of delivering the guarantee that they want to have. It usually just means you can't do it today. Find a way to make it happen and stop making excuses.

The other myth and the biggest myth is that they're terrified that somebody's going to rip them off. And you know what? Somebody is going to try and rip you off. Somebody is going to try and take advantage of your guarantee. The good news is, is that it's such a small percentage that you can factor that into your cost structure.

Remember FEAR is usually – False Expectations Appearing Real.

> **Why have a guarantee?**
>
> 1. It increases confidence. Confidence in you. Confidence in your products and your services.
>
> 2. It give absolute security. It gives security for you because you know that you have to live up to a particular standard. But it gives security to the customer and the client that you're dealing with that they know that they know they're going to get what they pay for.
>
> 3. It reduces risk. If you can eliminate risk even better. But if you can't eliminate risk, reduce the risk because there's more than just monetary risk.

It is a contract that you agree to give to your clients the right things in the right time frame in the right manner, the right product that they expect.

It builds trust because ultimately you need to trust the person or the company that you're dealing with.

> Very few people will buy purely based on price unless they don't feel trust and confidence in all areas within your business. – John Millar

"Sometimes it's better to spend a little bit too much and lose a little than to spend too little and lose everything." – Anon

> Remember. There's no use being different for difference's sake. – John Millar

> You need to actually have some quality behind that difference.

> You must make sure that your guarantee is meaningful. That it's not overly complex but it has a requirement for both parties to do the right things.

Often we can learn by the mistakes of others so that we can do positive things ourselves.
-John Millar

A suspect is somebody who fits the criteria of your perfect customer but you've not met them yet. You don't know them. They don't know you. They fit your target market but you haven't actually come across each other.

> Who is your target market?

1.
2.
3.
4.
5.

> Who are the segments, the niches, the groups, the demographics that are actually going to suit you and your business goals and that's what makes up your suspect list?

1. _____
_____
_____

2. _____
_____
_____

3. _____
_____
_____

4. _____
_____
_____

5. _____
_____
_____

> Niches are getting smaller and smaller and smaller, so having a single target market is a really important thing to actually have in today's market. – John Millar

_____
_____
_____
_____

Can you have several niche markets? Absolutely, but make sure that they are specific niche markets.

_____
_____
_____
_____

We're after both market share and wallet share.

What do I mean by market share and wallet share?

> Making sure that we get clients coming back and spending more, and more often and retained is what changes it from wallet share to market share. – John Millar

When we differentiate our customers it not as simply enough to break it down to those chunks of who are they? Where do they come from? Where do they live? What are their demographics? What do they like to buy? When do they like to buy?

> You must look at the quality of your clients and grade them accordingly to what is important to you, your business, your team and your vision / mission.
>
> – John Millar

How do we actually then grade those customers?

> The Pareto Principle as applied to business states that 80% of your profit is probably coming from 20% of your clients and 80% of your headaches are probably coming from 20% of your clients. With this in mind why not focus your attentions on those 20% that are producing 80% of your profits and strive to get more like them? Likewise, wouldn't it make sense to improve or remove the 20% of your customers that are causing 80% of your problems? – John Millar

Have you broken it down to an A, B, C and D customer?

> An "A" grade customer is an Awesome customer. They pay in full. They pay on time. They come back regularly. They ask you what else that you have available that they can get. They tell as many people – their friends and family and associates, they can, all about you. These are the people that you want to treat like family.

A "B" grade client is really a Basic customer. These are at least consistent in their purchases with you. They're your worker bee-type customers. They just come in, they're probably not going to tell too many people about you. They aren't really going to quibble about price. They don't really do much of anything. They just come in just and buy business from you. We want to be able to step these people from B's to A's.

The "C" grade clients are the ones you just Can't deal with.

I really believe that the day you think a particular customer shouldn't be doing business with you anymore is the day that you should be introducing them to your competitor. – John Millar

"C" grade clients are the people that suck up your time, never pay their invoices on time. Complain about deliveries being two seconds late. Are completely inflexible in what they want compared to what you can deliver. Change their mind on what they're doing. They're constant dramas. They hunt in packs so any referral you ever get from them is going to be just as bad.

> Send them and their mates packing. Send them to your competitors and let them enjoy dealing with the customers that you just can't deal with and you really shouldn't deal with. – John Millar

Under my consulting and mentoring and coaching programs, you need to apply for me to work with you one on one. It's really important that I do that because I need to be certain that not only do you want to business with me, but I want to do business with you. I won't deal with C and D grade customers. And in fact, I'll be loath to take on B grade clients. I'm more interested in A grade awesome clients with good businesses that want to become great businesses.

> You need to have the courage and conviction to make sure that you're running your business the way you need to, without sacrificing some of the other areas of your life, wallet and sanity that are important. – John Millar

> A "D" grade customer is dead. They're gone. They've gone elsewhere. They're never coming back. They've moved. They could be part of that very small percentage of people that do actually die. They are probably sitting on your customer list, assuming you even have one, but they are never coming back to do business with you again so clean it up.

Now we know what you do, how you do it, what makes you special and who your target market REALLY is we are now ready to start looking at where are we going to go and find our customers.

What are we going to tell them in your marketing and advertising?

So often I see marketing and advertising campaigns and pieces where the what is so confusing because they're trying to tell you 10 different things at once.

> Keep it simple, stupid.

I was once told uh, by a mentor of mine many years ago that the what needs to be simple enough to be quickly understood by an 8 year old.

Stop throwing multiple messages at people. Keep it clear.

Remember: No one likes to be sold anything but everybody loves to buy what they want. – John Millar

Other questions you need to consider are:

Why do they want to buy what you have?

....
....
....

Why do they want to invest their time, their money and themselves and in investing themselves with you, your products and your services?

....
....
....

What are the features that you're offering that are going to offer them the benefits that are going to be most satisfactory to them?

....
....
....
....

> Remember: It's got nothing to do with how good it makes you feel. It's all about how it makes them feel. – John Millar

....
....
....
....

How are you going to communicate the offer to them?

....
....

Is it going to be online and if so what's your online marketing plan?

Is it going to be offline and if so what is your offline marketing plan?

Is it going to be highly repetitive and if so what is it you need to keep repeating to be heard?

Is it going to have a mixed message? Singular message?

Is it on your website?

Is it on a regular newsletter?

> Is it on FaceBook? Is it on Twitter? Is it on LinkedIn, Google ad words? Is it maximizing your search optimization?

Spend the bulk of your time writing ads that focus on your target, about half of your remaining time on the offer and then the balance on the copy.

On average we find that about 4% of your target market are ready to buy from you today or from one of your competitors.

The other 96% are people that are potentially your target market are looking passively for reasons to do business with you when the opportunity is right but are not ready today.

Your marketing needs to look at building the image and building the opportunity that when they're ready to buy that they immediately recall you.

> Ask yourself the question: "What am I doing to build my image today to elicit as positive a response immediately. But also get that lifetime value from my advertising so that product recall is absolutely spot on."

Marketing is designed to catch their attention and then to develop a sincere desire to do business with you.

Make them hungry for it and then create a call to action that means that they need to do it right now.

> Look at your own web page and others, grab your local paper some magazines. I want you to go through it and just run through a quick exercise and have a look at what actually works. Pick out the things that catch your attention.

Does it develop a level of interest within you? Does it create a desire that you must have it right now?

There are some real cardinal rules when you're actually creating a headline but one of the most important and widely abused is people who put your own name in the headline.

The only person who ever wants to see your Business name and your name in the headline is you and your mother.

Make sure that you put the word you in it that actually makes it personal.

Make sure that you're actually qualifying the right readers so that when they call you your qualification period has already begun.

You're actually working through what we call a process of de-selection. And that de-selecting is allowing them to de-select themselves from giving you a call. Giving you time the resources and the energy to focus on those you really need to give focus to.

Make sure that you're selling the benefits of doing business with you.

Make sure that the headline takes up somewhere between 20 and 25% of the space in the ad.

Remember, the ad is not going to be able to transact a credit card, bank a cheque or take cash for you. The ad is really there to elicit a response. Whether that response is to pick up a phone and call you, walk in your door or go to your website to send you an e-mail.

> Don't try and oversell. Give people the opportunity to buy from you.

Make sure in printed material that the layout and the picture are appropriate.

> Make sure that if you do place a photograph of a person, that the photograph is placed within the top third of the shot. Remember, people like to buy from people, and for goodness sake don't just show your head. Include your head and shoulders at the very least.

You can have a great ad in the right publication, but just have it in the wrong position. Always make sure you are in the first 10 pages of any publication and that you are on the right hand page and towards the top of that page. Make sure that you've got a headline at the top and your name and contact details at the bottom. They need to be able to get a hold of you.

W-I-I-F-M. What's In It For Me?

It's not about what you want to sell them, it's what they want you to assist them to buy. – John Millar

Make sure that you use a very simple font.

We want to create a great offer. We want to use sizzling words.

> The call to action must be specific. It must be easy. It must be time bound. It must be driven within some boundaries that allow people to take action, whenever possible, particularly that 4%, right now.

> Get this right and you will frolic in marketing heaven. Get this wrong and you'll be languishing in marketing hell.

I look forward to hearing more about the exciting changers inside your business and seeing you at one of our workshops, seminars, training sessions or coaching and mentoring programs so that you can make More Profit in Less Time.

John Millar

Keep this page blank for photocopying

7 Steps to More Profit Less Time

Area	Current Figure	Areas of Potential	Increase	New Forecast
Number of Enquiries				
×			×	
Conversion %				
=			=	
New Customers				
+			+	
Retained Customers				
=			=	
Total Customer Base				
×			×	
Average $ Sale				
×			×	
Average of Transaction				
=			=	
Total Revenue				
×			×	
Average GP Margin %				
=			=	
Total Gross Profit				
−			−	
Fixed Costs				
=			=	
Net Profit				

Business Essentials Series...

Disc 1 in the Business Essentials Series
Gaining Focus in Your Business
This is about your fundamental learning skills and what you will need to do to change them to vastly improve the way you look
at your development to become a truly effective business owner not just simply remain self-employed.

You will also give you some excellent tools to set goals, work on your plans and create a diary that will allow you to steal your time back to begin moving your business from chaos to control.

Disc 2 in the Business Essentials Series
Getting Your Financials Right
You will learn the importance of understanding your financials.

After all being in business is about making profit and having cash flow work for YOU since you are responsible for your profits.
Become your accountant and book keepers best friend by understanding more about how the financials in your business works so you can ask them better questions to maximise your profits not simply ensure tax compliance.

Disc 3 in the Business Essentials Series
Leveraging Your Business Harder
You will learn the principles of what and how to leverage far more in your business to get more from less and to work far smarter and not just harder.

Here is where you will receive some of the tools you will need to better understand how to get your business flying, what it is you need to test and measure, how to do it and WHY it's so important.

Disc 4 in the Business Essentials Series
How to Generate More Clients Profitably
This is where you will determine your uniqueness, develop a meaningful guarantee and learn the basics of good advertising.

You will gain a better appreciation between the difference of Marketing and Advertising, learn how to get the most for the least investment and ensure that you do it all profitably.

Disc 5 in the Business Essentials Series
Maximising Your Conversion Rates
Get to know how your Sales Pipeline REALLY works and how to identify who your suspects really are, convert prospects into regular shoppers and understand how much more work you can do to maximise your sales experience.

Disc 6 in the Business Essentials Series
Meet and Exceed Your Clients Expectations
Now you have new customers, how do you make sure you KEEP them, how do you wanting to come back time and again while telling their friends? ...this is where you really make a difference.

Disc 7 in the Business Essentials Series
Systemising Your Business For Consistent Excellence
Do you recognise the importance of having systems in your business and how they can improve your profitability?

We show you how to systemise like a corporate while retaining the culture of a smaller business. Understanding how we systemise for routine and humanise for the exceptions will enable you to be the best in your field every time.

Disc 8 in the Business Essentials Series
Do You Have a Champion Team with a Champion Leader?
This is about having the right people on the bus. It starts with you however so you'll learn how to maximise your own skills and then you will attract and retain the right people.

When you understand how the TEAM is the most important part of your business and what needs to be done to achieve the very best from yourselves and others you are well on your way to becoming a better manager of this invaluable resource.

Disc 9 in the Business Essentials Series
The Essentials of Getting Your Time Back.
This is where you get to redefine your time management You will understand better how you can start working far more on the business than in the business than ever before.

You will also finally find out why others can seem to fit more into their day while having a great LIFE – WORK balance (notice the order!)..

Disc 10 in the Business Essentials Series
Simply Brilliant Customer Service.
It's so easy to give mediocre or good customer service but it's just as easy to give amazing service to your customers and delight them.

You will understand the simple easy steps that you must take to provide consistently brilliant service and how to get your team excited about doing it.

Disc 11 in the Business Essentials Series
Discovering DISC and EQ not just IQ.
We believe for things to change first you must change so here you will learn why you behave as you do and just as importantly understand why other people react and act the way they do.

You will also learn what DISC really is and what it isn't. You will learn how to apply these important principles in your recruitment and team management / development.

You will learn how to use these ideas in creating a more dynamic team and discover the what and why of emotional intelligence. You will also develop key strategies for using the knowledge here and the tools we have available on our website and why we place such a massive emphasis on DISC and other tools that support, train and develop your team.

You will also learn how to use these skills and observations at home and socially not just at the workplace.

Disc 12 in the Business Essentials Series
Quality Recruitment.
Recruitment of the right people for the right reasons in the right roles for your team is so incredibly important yet so often ignored or pushed to the rear.

You will learn who the right person is for your business and the role you want filled.
You will be able to identify the right people early in the process to save yourself and them the time and money wasted with antique recruitment methodologies that just don't work anymore.

How to get the best out of your recruitment activities so you can keep the assets you acquire for the long term and get the best return from your investment.

ABOUT THE AUTHOR

John Millar is the Managing Director, Senior Business Coach Trainer and Consultant with More Profit Less Time Pty Ltd and CEO-ONDEMAND. Along with his many other business interests, John is proud to have been an associate of the most successful coaching team in the world.

He is recognized as a global leader and has been benchmarked against over 1,300 colleagues in 31 countries. John has over 25 years of hands-on ownership, management, coaching, and entrepreneurial experience in a broad range of industry sectors, including retail, wholesale, import, export, IT, trades and trade services, automotive, primary production, food services, transport, manufacturing, mining, professional services, the fitness industry, and more.

He has extensive experience developing and providing training for small to medium-sized companies and a variety of publicly listed corporate companies. John is an accomplished and talented public and professional speaker. He has been a mentor working with sales/management activities for businesses with a turnover under $100,000 per annum, over $100 million turnover, and everything in between, with great success.

John currently works with business owners and their teams across Australia and has a "Whatever it takes" attitude that has enabled him to help his clients grow their business profits by up to 800%.

If you are ready to be coached by one of the best in the business, register at:

www.ceo-ondemand.com.au

Make sure to visit www.moreprofitlesstime.com for the new online Management Development Program: The Business Essentials Series.

ACCLAIM FOR JOHN MILLAR'S
Business Coaching and Training in their own words...

"Without John Millar as my Business Coach I wouldn't have a business today."—Grant Jennings Managing Director, Jigsaw Projects

"Taking the decision to be coached and trained by John Millar was carefully considered after experiencing those who over promised and under delivered. I am pleased to say the content of his courses are the tools we all need to master as business owners. His delivery is engaging, thought provoking and empowering and after every session l came away re-energised. John always makes himself available for business building advice both via Skype and face to face beyond the scope of delivery. With his extensive personal experience in building small businesses, he knows and understands what it takes to establish and grow a business. I have no hesitation endorsing John Millar as an educator and business coach and the bonus is he is a very nice person."—Anne Lederman Managing Director FB Salons"

Johns training with my management team was excellent, it was very different from the business coaching and support I have had in the past. John was clear, thoughtful and he addressed the issues we needed to cover without us even knowing they were being addressed! His follow up has been fantastic and exactly what I needed. I would recommend John and his team to anyone looking at getting some business coaching and training done" —Wendy Crawford, Peopleworx

"In my dealings with John as our business coach, I have found him to be a motivated and insightful agent of positive change. He is able to burrow down to the root cause of issues and introduce effective forms of measurement. John then identifies and implements practical solutions and is there to provide the gentle persuasion required to ensure that results are achieved." —Mark Felton, Lindale Insurances

"You have coached and trained us so well throughout the year that we are now used to & find it easy to prepare a 90 day plan, then breaks it down to actionable bite size pieces. Planning in business & personal life certainly is important. It allows us to identify the important things & the bigger picture. Thank you for your support & guidance throughout the year. And not to mention your insight, external perspective to review & assist our business moving forward." —Linda Turner, Director Roy A McDonald Certified Practicing Accountants

"If you want to achieve sales results you never thought were possible and give yourself a competitive edge my strong suggestion is to engage John services and listen closely to what John has to say, during the time I was trained by John I was one of eight sales consultants in a national business for 10 out of the 13 months I lead the sales tally and in 1 quarter I generated three times the revenue of the national sales force combined. Johns training and experience was well worth the investment and paid big dividends. Thanks John." —Julian Fadini, Bellvue Capital

"John is a very enthusiastic trainer and business coach, he is very passionate about getting business owners and their team where they need to be. He goes the extra mile to keep ahead of the latest developments which he then uses to benefit his clients." —Darren Reddy CPA

"I have been to a few seminars and heard John speak numerous times about sales, marketing and business. He is a very knowledgeable and extremely enthusiastic business coach in all his interactions and I would recommend him to all business owners who need a sales and marketing boost!" —Andrew Heath, Managing Director, Fresh Living Group

"I worked with John Millar and found his business knowledge, passion and innovation to be inspiring. He has always been able to set (and achieve) strategic long and short-term goals both for himself and his clients without losing that personal connection he builds with everyone he meets. He has been and I believe will continue to be a strong mentor and trainer for anyone wanting to take that next step in their business." —Bree Webster, Online Marketing Guru

"Massive Action Day" – what an understatement, John Millars 4 hour frenzy challenged me to seriously review areas of my business I would not have gone to .... In this way, the process identified incongruence's in my mind, my business and my modus operandi. It's created a paradigm shift. Thanks John, the road map just got a whole lot clearer. Your friendship and insights since 2003 have been a gift to my business and I." —Andrew Reay, Counsellor, Hypnotherapist and Counsellor, Thinkshift Transformations

"John Millar is not your usual Business coach or trainer; he gets involved with you and your business and provides hands on help to make sure you follow through on his advice. He is highly motivated to help his clients and his personal guarantee certainly shows this. He has now transposed his thoughts, advice and love of good business onto a series of DVD's in his business venture – More Profit Less Time. This has excellent tips and advice for anyone either starting out or already in business. I highly recommend John to any business owner who wants to run a business and not a j.o.b.!" —Darren Cassidy, Managing Director HR2U

"I and many of my Business Partners and colleagues have worked with John since 2010 as our business oath, trainer and motivator and found him to be an extremely motivational person to assist us achieve our business goals. This company and its products allows for John's skill set to be accessed by a wider number of potential clients. His very professional DVD series is extremely good value for money and is easily accessible for all of us who are time poor. If you are looking to maximise your and your business's results and to start achieving your goals and dreams, contact John; you won't look back!!" —Mark Cleland, Mortgage Choice

"John develops real relationships with the people he comes into contact with. He is pasionate about what he does. His DVD and group training series, is full of good ideas and process to make your business better. Knowing what to do and actually doing it are two different things. John is excellent at helping you get things done." —Carey Rudd, Sales Director, Online Knowledge

"I have known John since 2004 and found him to be extremely knowledgably in both Sales and Business systems as a business coach without peer. John has provided me with business advice as well as personal coaching over the years, helping me with the running of my organisation. I'm impressed with John's DVD series where he has condensed a lot of the information in an easy to follow format that any business owner can use immediately. I wish he had released these DVDs earlier, as they are a goldmine of information, and practical how to that allow anyone to increase the profit in their business and get back valuable wasted time." —Steve Psaradellis, Managing Director, TEBA

"John's DVD and workbook delivery of his no-nonsense advice provides a low-cost option for those business owners looking to set and achieve goals that will increase profit. I found the conversational style of the DVD's easy to follow, whilst the requirement to pause the DVD and write down some action points ensured a level of commitment to the advice being provided." — Mark Felton, Lindale Insurances

"I only met John briefly at a BNI meeting and knew instantly i need to hire him for my business as my business coach. His attitude towards work and how to improve my cash line had an instant effect on before, even before I finally hired him on an official basis. I found myself thinking "what would John do" and this was only after just meeting him. I cannot see my business expend and give me "More Profit Less Time" without John's expert direction and training. If you want to succeed in business life, you need John Millar, without him you're just kidding yourself " —Leslie Cachia, Managing Director, Letac Drafting

"I can highly recommend John Millar to any business owner who wants to grow his business. When I hear very positive feedback from colleagues who are skeptics by nature about John's ability and skills, I know John will help all those he comes in contact with. John comes with a selfless nature and the willingness to work inside a client's business to make it succeed. Rare indeed!" —Darren Cassidy, Managing Director, HR2U"I first met John Millar in mid-2010 and have always found him to be of an honest and generous character that engenders an easy association with him. I love how easy he is to listen to and how passionate he is about his work and topics. John demonstrates a love for life and his work and I have no hesitation in recommending his services." —Kathie M Thomas, Managing Director, VA

"I have listened to John speak on a number of occasions and find him a very knowledgeable speaker with a passion for what he does. I have also interacted with a number of his clients and they all tell me that he helps them achieve results in their business. If you are looking for business help John is a person you can trust." —Carey Rudd, Sales Director, Online Knowledge

"John knows his stuff, he knows how the get results, John has so many great ideas in building a business and helping business owners work less and make more money. John has released a DVD set on doing just that. I have watched the 1st one and it was great, very informative and easy to understand, I happily recommend John to anyone in need of help and guidance" —Frank Eramo, Proprietor, Dynotune

"I have known John only for a short time, however the impact that he has had on me, not just my business has helped me to visualise opportunities that I began to doubt my ability to realise. He is encouraging and at the same time challenging so that he can/you can, begin to see how to maximise the business potential, John calls it being an unreasonable friend, I call it being a mate. If you have any questions about the direction of your business, if you want to seem your bottom line improve not just turnover but real profit, if you want a person who will work with you then I strongly recommend that you engage him at your earliest convenience. John is the best thing that has happened to my business. I could tell you about the way he is on track to make 1/2 a million for me on his contacts alone, but that actually sells him short, he has become like my partner in business, and cares about my success as if it was his own, we will flourish because I took the step to employ his training to help me grow. If you get a chance to get him training you, don't wait like I did, get in as quickly as possible, his time is your business and if like me your business is to make money, then every day you don't have him on retainer you lose money." —Russell Summers, Managing Director, The Give Life Centre

"It's usually easy to be mediocre in business but it's impossible when you have John Millar training you. He has been my right hand since 2003!" —David Manser, CFO, Hydrosteer

"I now have a commercial, profitable business and now it's my choice when I work IN my business and when I work ON it and have had john helping me in business since 1988. I can't imagine not having John as a part of our business." —David Wall, Director, D&K Transport

"The work John has done since 2008 coaching and training our marketing team, administration and finance teams, buyers, store managers and staff nationally have been fantastic." —Ross Sudano, Director, Anaconda Adventure Stores

"John is a creative, professional, practical and committed business coach and trainer. His approach since we first met him in 1994 to working with a client team through the application of useful tools, information and anecdotes along with his easy going & easy to understand delivery sets him apart from other business coaches that I have used in the past." —Anthony Beasley, Director, The Astra Group

"I have worked with John Millar for the since 2004 and I didn't think it was possible to achieve what we have achieved together. His business coaching, training and services just get better and better!" —Terrance Chong, Managing Director, Echo Graphics and Printing

"John's business coaching, training and support has transformed our business across Australia and New Zealand since 2008."—Rose Vis, Managing Director, VIP Australia

"We first met John in 2005, he is AMAZING at sales, marketing, operations, logistics, finance training and so much more. Since engaging John as our business coach our business has exploded, our team are happy, our clients are raving about us and my husband and I now take at least 12 weeks holidays a year, EVERY year." —Shirley Du, Director, Goldline Technology

"It's the no nonsense results driven business coaching and training focus John bought to the table that had such a massive effect on our business." —David Runkel, Director, Tracomp Fabrication and Steel

"We started working with John in early 2010, within 90 days of working with and being trained by John Millar we had the biggest and most profitable month in our 15 year history. That's impressive." —Hugh Gilchrist, Managing Director, Australian Moulding Company

"If you don't have John as your business trainer you aren't meeting your business potential." —Don Robertson, Director, Medallion Electrical Services

Thank You

www.ingramcontent.com/pod-product-compliance
Lightning Source LLC
Chambersburg PA
CBHW050817180526
45159CB00004B/1702